Families

Role Models

Rebecca Rissman

www.raintreepublishers.co.uk

Visit our website to find out
more information about
Raintree books.

To order:

☎ Phone 0845 6044371

🖨 Fax +44 (0) 1865 312263

💻 Email myorders@raintreepublishers.co.uk

Customers from outside the UK please telephone +44 1865 312262

Raintree is an imprint of Capstone Global Library Limited, a
company incorporated in England and Wales having its registered
office at 7 Pilgrim Street, London, EC4V 6LB – Registered
company number: 6695582

Edited by Rebecca Rissman, Dan Nunn, and Catherine Veitch
Designed by Ryan Frieson
Picture research by Tracy Cummins
Production by Victoria Fitzgerald
Originated by Capstone Global Library
Printed and bound in China by Leo Paper Products Ltd

ISBN 978 1 406 22150 3
14 13 12 11 10
10 9 8 7 6 5 4 3 2 1

British Library Cataloguing in Publication Data
Rissman, Rebecca.
Role models. -- (Families)
306.8'7-dc22

Acknowledgements
We would like to thank the following for permission to reproduce
photographs:
Corbis pp. 5 (©Grady Reese), 10 (Don Mason), 14 and 23 middle
(both Tim Pannell); Getty Images pp. 4 (Anthony Plummer),
8 (Sami Sarkis), 11 (Michael Regan), 12 (Uwe Krejci), 13
(Bambu Productions), 15 (Jim Bastardo), 17 (Paul Chesley), 18
(Keith Brofsky), 20 (Zoran Milich), 21 (Chip Somodevilla), 22
(Absodels), 23 bottom (Keith Brofsky), 23 top (Zoran Milich);
istockphoto p. 7 (©digitalskillet); Photolibrary pp. 16 (Joeleen
Pryhitko), 19 (Colin Hawkins); Shutterstock pp. 6 (©Alena
Brozova), 9 (©bikeriderlondon).

Front cover photograph of master instructing a student in a
tae kwon do class reproduced with permission of Getty Images
(LWA). Back cover photograph of mother and child reproduced
with permission of Shutterstock (©Alena Brozova).

We would like to thank Nancy Harris, David and Diana [...] in the preparation of this book.

Every effort has been made to contact copyright holders of material reproduced in this book. Any omissions will be rectified in subsequent printings if notice is given to the publisher.

Contents

What is a family?

A family is a group of people who care for each other.

People in families are called
family members.

All families are different.

All families are special.

What are families like?

Families can be loud.

Families can be quiet.

What is a role model?

Role models are leaders.

People want to do what the
leader does.

Role models set a good example.

They show others how to do the right thing.

Role models in the family

Family members can be role models.

Parents can be role models.

Brothers and sisters can be
role models.

Grandparents can be role models.

Role models outside of the family

Teachers can be role models.

Friends can be role models.

Coaches can be role models.

Leaders can be role models.

Your role model

Do you have a role model?

Can you be a role model?

Picture glossary

coach person who helps others learn about a sport or game

member person who belongs to a group

teacher person who helps others to learn. Teachers often work at schools.

Index

Note to parents and teachers

Before reading

Write "Leader" and "Good Example" on the board, and ask children to come up with descriptive words for each. Record the descriptors under the two words. Then discuss how a good role model is a good leader and sets a good example.

After reading

Ask children to make a poster showing a role model they know. Encourage them to cut out words and pictures from magazines that help describe their role model. Then ask children to turn their poster over, and use the opposite side for a role model they don't know, such as a political leader. Encourage them to use magazine clippings on this poster as well.